HUNTING ADVENTURES WITH MY DADDY

by Ben Brookhart

Illustrated by Judy Siler Boyette

Hunting Adventures with My Daddy
Copyright © 2021 Ben Brookhart

All rights reserved. No part of this publication may be reproduced, distributed, or transmitted in any form or by any means, including photocopying, recording, or other electronic or mechanical methods, without the prior written permission of the publisher, except in the case of brief quotations embodied in critical reviews and certain other noncommercial uses permitted by copyright law. Permission requests should be sent to info@writewaypublishing.com.

Printed in the United States of America
ISBN 978-1-956543-00-1 softcover
ISBN 978-1-956543-02-5 hardcover

Book Design by CSinclaire Write-Design
Illustrations by Judy Siler Boyette © Ben Brookhart

an imprint of WriteWay Publishing LLC

• For Jack and Adam •

*We've had some great hunting adventures!
I love spending time with both of you in the woods
and can't wait to see what the next hunting adventure will be.
I love you both so much and thank you
for being my hunting buddies!*

What could it be?
What do you see?
CLUES: It's brown.
It has a bushy white tail.
And big antlers!

What could it be?
What do you see?
CLUES: It is grey and white and runs in a pack.

Off to **UTAH** we go to hunt an animal you may know.

What could it be?
What do you see?
CLUES: It has tan fur, big paws, and it can climb trees!

What could it be?
What do you see?
CLUES: It's BIG with brown fur, a long nose, and big claws.

to see what we can see.

What could it be?
What do you see?
CLUES: It has scaly skin, a long tail, and it can float in the water.

Off to **NORTH CAROLINA** we go to hunt an animal you may know.

What could it be?
What do you see?
CLUES: It has two feet, lots of feathers, and a long beard.

Goodnight, Mr. Whitetail Buck!

Goodnight, Mr. Grey Wolf!

Goodnight, Mr. Mountain Lion!

Goodnight, Mr. Alligator!

Goodnight, Mr. Grizzly Bear!

Goodnight, Mr. Tom Turkey!

www.ingramcontent.com/pod-product-compliance
Lightning Source LLC
Chambersburg PA
CBHW040001290426
43673CB00077B/296